THE GLASS IS ALREADY BROKEN

Poems & Essays of Love, Life & Loss

Carol deSchryver Walkner

To Suzanne
I am so grateful
you are in my
life

Love,
Carol

ISBN-10: 1727735676
ISBN-13: 9781727735673

See all of my books at: CarolWalkner.com

Cover design by Nick Zelinger, NZGraphics.com

Internal design, typesetting, and photography
by Maggie Pund @MaggiePund

For Ryan, my son who I love beyond measure; for Joy, my sister, my confidant, my dear friend; and for Women Writing For (a) Change, the writing school founded by Mary Pierce Brosmer, where my writing took flight.

"Poetry is not only dream and vision; it is the skeleton architecture of our lives. It lays the foundations for a future of change, a bridge across our fears of what has never been before."

Audra Lord

"Barn's burnt down, now I can see the moon."

Mizuta Masahide

PREFACE

One day, some people came to the Thai Buddhist meditation master and asked, "How can you be so happy in a world of such impermanence?" The master held up a glass and said, "Someone gave me this glass, and I really like this glass. It holds my water admirably, and it glistens in the sunlight. I touch it, and it rings! One day the wind may blow it off the shelf or my elbow may knock it from the table. And I say, 'Of course.' When I understand that the glass is already broken, every moment with it is precious."

When we realize that change is inevitable and that nothing lasts forever, then we are less likely to be devastated when something ends, breaks, falls apart, crumbles, or gets ripped away from us. Does it hurt? Of course! Are we stunned, shocked? Yes, totally. Are we devastated? Possibly...*but not permanently*. Instead of becoming immobilized when something is destroyed, ends, or changes, we'll be able to feel grateful for the time we had with it – the job, the relationship, the life experience, that beautiful thing.

As Pema Chödrön reminds us, "seasons stand up to testify to the fact that everything is in a state of constant change. An ordinary state of affairs." Embracing impermanence can fill our lives with reverence for who we are, what we have, and what we do every day. In the immortal words of Dr. Seuss, "Don't cry because it's over. Smile because it happened."

Impermanence...breathe it in.
Exhale gratitude for who you are and what you have.
Now breathe in gratitude and exhale impermanence.
Now just breathe...

The glass is already broken.

CONTENTS

LIFE IS DELICIOUS!

DELICIOUS!

I swallow the lightning
    then can turn to dust
        what's wrong in the world.
I digest the thunder
    and my voice breaks
        your eardrums.
The rain drops slide down
    my throat, fill me up,
        drown my screams.
Each new snowflake alights
    on my head, one by one
        turning my words delicious!
Turning all of me delicious!

THE OLD METAL ROLLER SKATE

It's right here!
Right where I left it!
Eons ago
  or yesterday.
Now where is
the key? Find the key!
  and the world
  is mine!

SHE'S GONE BUT NOT FORGOTTEN

Where is she?
That confident 9-year-old, vivid
stranger. She's calling to me.
Did she disappear
in a puff of smoke? Or drift
up to the atmosphere to become
one with the clouds,
turn to rain, to fall in grand
drops, invisible on the asphalt,
evaporating as soon as
the sun comes out.
Where is she?

MUSIC SEEN

It's like hearing voices,
seeing the notes dance
on the other side of your
eyes as the sly ones steal
into your night and take
what you do not want to
give. Your hands are tied.
The voices say go ahead;
the notes cry in anguish
for your vanquished other
dreams. What will you do
with what is left?

SAVOUR...

the moment, appreciate it all fully,
seeing this minute, standing alone
with your heart in your eyes,
your soul close by, sublimely aware,
eating your ice cream cone with gusto.

DISEASES...

some happen when you swallow
your sadness whole,
ziplock your lips
and don't speak your truth
crying only on the inside
where no one can see.

THOUGHTS...

weave around and through
        my brain like
           campfire smoke
   easily blown away by the
endless to do lists of nothing
    that really matters.

WHEN YOUR DREAMS...

turn to dust...
      vacuum
    but
  never empty the
bag!

CONFUSION...

that state
when the heart
the head and
the feet are all
going in different
directions
at the same time
and it tears you
apart.

on my

turning my words

delicious!

RELATIONSHIP
STEW

RELATIONSHIP STEW RECIPE...

2   quarts love
2   cups myself
3   cups you
5   cups everyone else
3   Tbsp joy
2   Tbsp anger (this will change with age – more or less)
6   tsp keeping your mouth shut
1   cup speaking up
4   Tbsp respect
2   cups anguish
1   cup fear
2   cups faith
5   Tbsp depression

Mix all ingredients together.
Add salt and pepper, frowns, giggles and smiles to taste.
Bring to a boil in early childhood.
Cook throughout adulthood.
Turn to low and simmer throughout old age.

ODE TO THE YOUNGER SISTER

I want you to notice me,
    play with me, see me please.
Know that I am here and
    I love you more than
        you could imagine.
You have your own friends; you
    are almost five years older
than I am so that makes me
    an annoying little gnat,
        crawling up your arm.
A tiny bug that you want to swat at,
    flick off into space, something to
        unsee
        unrealize
        unacknowledge
        unknow

I think you love me. I see *you.* I see
    your heart ride up into your eyes
on those rare occasions when you
    look in my direction. I cherish
        that look, that moment.
I blow it out of proportion so that I can
    bear to keep going for one more day.
        I know you.
You helped me learn how to ride a bike
    so that I could ride away from you
instead of ride with you.
You play kickball in the street; you
    roller skate until the sky turns dark
        and you can barely see your toes
sticking out of the ends of your skates.

I know you.
know you
no
you

I know you are out there in the world
and I am here in the house with
a mother who doesn't
see me either,
so I play with my dolls; I have
long conversations with a roomful
of imaginary friends. I am the
most popular one in that illusory crowd.
They know me.
they know
no
me

I want *you* to know me, my fair,
curly-haired older sister. I want you
to share your life with me –
a minute of your day, your baseball cards,
your 1000-watt smile. I want you
to know that I dream of horses,
of being at Grandma's house in the country,
of ice cream cones, red licorice and
of a mother who kisses
my forehead and tells me she
loves me.
loves
she
me

I want you to know me, know me.
        Know that my heart aches, know
                that my eyes refuse to
let one tear out. If one escapes
        the others will follow. They will fill
                all the oceans in all the
earth and then I wouldn't be able
        to see you. I would forget I know you.
                See me
                see me
                me.
                        see.
                                Please.

THE CONVERSATION

Her slender fingers
tipped glossy dark
rose-colored, held
the Pall Mall loosely.

She brought it slowly
to her thin magenta lips,
inhaled deeply as she
closed her eyes, tilted
her head back, temporarily
transported…

Leisurely, she opened her
eyes, exhaled, chuckled
deep in her throat and
finished her sentence to
my mother beside her.
The cigarette was rimmed
with a rosy dark circle.

My mother, with her shiny
candy apple nails, raised
her Kent Filtered King to
her lush, scarlet lips,
coughed deeply, took
a long drag, then asked,

Now what will you do?!

RYAN – THE SON, MOON AND STARS

I am your son and I want you to know me.
I forgive you for allowing my grandfather
to threaten you away, calling you crazy,
suicidal, unfit to be my mom. You believed
him; I didn't.

I want you to see me beyond your own pain,
your own loss of me to my loss of me
and you. I want you to know I dream
of spaceships, horses, flying, traveling
and you.

I was born from you, a part of your soul, your
heart, your very being and I am with
you always even when you can't see me.
I know you love me more than life, and
miss me,

much more than I miss you. I am good at getting
on with life, with a wife, kids, and work that
keeps me going around in circles so I
don't think of the years I am trying to
forget.

I am your son and you've known me forever.

GONE IN A BLINK

My little one was right there
in that spot on the playground
and I only turned away, blinked
at the backfiring car and then
back and he was gone! My heart
stopped beating; my stomach
lurched as I swiveled my head
around...where did he go?! How
could I let this happen; it was
only an instant, son! Where
are you? I cried out as I dashed
from the sandbox, to the
stand of trees, to the swings;
Son! Son! Where are you?!
I'm here, mom, working
in New York, married and
dreaming of a
          child of my own...

THE TWINS

Twin seeds, intertwined individuals
the same yet so very different.
She of the black hair, staring
straight ahead out of cloudy eyes
calmly seeing all the unseen,
imagining her own greatness.

Twin hearts, intertwined individuals
the same yet so very different.
He, fairer, the follower, always
turned towards her awake,
watching, fidgeting, on guard,
screaming for her to see him.

Twin souls, intertwined individuals
the same, yet so very different.
She with deep queenly knowing
lets the world come to her
in its own time.

Twin beings, intertwined individuals
the same, yet so very different.
He startles, pants, frowns, cries,
wakes when she cries, screams
to understand this strange light place.

Twin voices, intertwined individuals
the same, yet so very different.
Two newborn bobble-headed magical beings
screaming, vying, crying for food, dryness, attention.
Their brother, the wise three-year-old remarks,
"The twins are going apeshit again!"

ME AND MR. O

We have been together a really long time – Mr. O and I. He was my first at age 23. And even at 65, I can proudly say there have been no others. No others in all these 42 years. He is still going strong; he never misses a holiday, a special occasion or a grand event. He is always there for me whenever I need him.

I remember one summer we held a backyard party for the kids, but, of course, adults were there as well. We prepared virgin daiquiris* for the kids and not-so-virgin ones for the adults. Thanks to Mr. O, it was a great party and a fun event.

Then there was the phase in my life when I was eating a healthy mix of fruits, vegetables, various powders, flaxseed, and non-dairy beverage; all blended together into a thick drink.* They were delicious. I was fit. Mr. O helped make it all happen.

Here in the Northeast, the autumns come with the smell of the crisp, cooler air mixed with the acridness of burning leaves. Winter coats, boots and gloves replace the flip-flops, tank tops and bathing suits of the bygone warmer days.

With the change of seasons, there comes the change in foods; from backyard barbeques to slow-cooked oven meals that bring warmth to any kitchen. It's time for homemade chili and soups too. Everyone raves about my soups. They're a wonderful way to warm up a cold, grey Sunday afternoon. Mr. O has helped me make sure the vegetable soup* is always velvety, thick and delicious.

For Thanksgiving, I make cranberry sauce from scratch with fresh cranberries, sugar, the juice and zest of an orange, and a tipple of orange liqueur.* Yummy and always the perfect consistency thanks to Mr. O.

Throughout the years, I have moved many times. Mr. O has always come with me. No matter what I was doing, he was always right there for me.

We've been together for so long, through thick and thin, and all the ups and downs of life. Whatever was thrown at us, we could handle.

I don't know what I would do without my Oster blender! Here's to another 42 years for both of us!

*See recipes next. I lost my recipe book long ago. Concocted over the 42 blissful years.

VIRGIN DAIQUIRI AND NOT-SO-VERY-VIRGIN ALSO

8-10 ice cubes
¼ cup rum – for the not-so-very-virgin version (virgins don't get rum)
1 cup cran-raspberry juice
A splash of ginger-flavored soda

Chop the ice. Switch to stir. When the ice has broken into smaller chunks, place the other ingredients into the blender. Puree until smooth and finally frappe for a few seconds.

FIT FOR LIFE BREAKFAST DRINK

2 cups almond, coconut or hemp milk
¼ cup flaxseed
½ cup protein or whey mix – vary every other day
Fruits – also change each day for different flavors:
1 banana or apple
½ cup raspberries, strawberries, blueberries, melon
– whatever is in season. Could add carrots, celery,
beets as an additional vegetable boost

Place all ingredients into blender. Stir until sufficiently
blended, puree – then enjoy!

CRANBERRY SAUCE WITH A KICK

2 bags fresh cranberries – 12 ounces each
1 cup sugar
Zest and juice from 1 orange
¼ cup orange liqueur (optional)

Place one bag of cranberries; ½ cup sugar; some of the
orange zest and juice; and ⅛ cup liqueur into blender.
Grind, blend, and stir until ingredients are mixed together in
a rough consistency. Pour into bowl and prepare the second
batch. For a smaller crowd, make only one batch.
Refrigerate for a couple of hours. Can prepare and
refrigerate the day before.

SOUTHWEST STYLE CARROT YAM SOUP WITH CILANTRO

Recipe from Diane Carlson, The Conscious Gourmet

<u>Ingredients</u>

    1 medium onion, chopped
    2 teaspoons extra virgin olive oil
    1 pound jewel yams, chopped
    1 pound carrots, chopped
    2 teaspoons ground cumin
    Optional: 1 dried ancho chile, seeds removed
    ¼ bunch cilantro, chopped
    5-6 cups water
    Another ¼ bunch cilantro, chopped
    Sea salt to taste
    ⅛ teaspoon cayenne pepper (if not using ancho)
    Fresh lemon juice or umeboshi plum vinegar to taste
    Chopped cilantro garnish

<u>Procedure</u>

Heat oil in a 3-quart soup pot. Add onions. Sauté until soft. Add carrots and yams. Sauté until vegetables sweat. Add cumin. Sauté 1 minute. Add ¼ bunch chopped cilantro. Add water (and optional ancho chile), bring to a boil, lower heat and simmer for 15 min. Add the remaining cilantro. Continue to cook until vegetables are soft.

If using the ancho chile, remove and discard, or for a spicier soup add the chili or a portion of it to the blender. Puree the soup in batches, returning puree to a clean soup pot. For a more textured soup, blend only one third of the soup. Add additional water to reach desired consistency. Add cayenne pepper, additional salt and lemon juice, or umeboshi vinegar to taste. Serve garnished with additional cilantro.

24

MY MOM AS CHEERLEADER...

My mom is not a cheerleader...
    no short skirt, pom-poms, loud
    voice, exuberance for 10 people
    jumping up and down for a crowd.
Oh, no, my mom is not a cheerleader.

My mom is a literati, a bookworm, an
    intellectual. She was a legal secretary,
    a loyal worker at a university, a wife,
    mother, friend and so much more.
Oh, no, my mom was never a cheerleader.

She is quiet, a little shy, soft spoken unless
    politics comes up. She wears long skirts
    and sweater sets in neutral colors with
    low-heeled shoes. She works her magic
behind the scenes, not seeking fame or recognition.

My mom's long black hair, turned grey, is permed to
    tight perfection; her snapping midnight
    blue eyes are filled with intelligence, love
    and forgiveness with a hint of resignation.
My mom has been gone for over 20 years.

In my mind's eye she is right beside me...
    cheering me on with her own kind of pom-pom,
    her silent excitement for life, her gentle voice
    whispering in my ear...encouraging me, loving me
cheering, cheering for me. My mom is *my* cheerleader!

THOSE
"WONDERFUL"
TEEN YEARS

and the world will offer itself to you

ISOLATION

I	I feel alone.
S	Soul disintegrating, heart breaking
O	On this other side of midnight.
L	Late in the dark, the moon smiles
A	And I cannot see through the endless
T	Tears from my eyes; tears in the fabric of my being.
I	I feel alone – at least I feel something,
O	On this endless day of days.
N	Nothingness descends as the sun rises.

INCLUSION

I   I am not alone anymore.
N   No one is shunning me.
C   Calm on the outside, nerve endings twanging inside,
L   Listening to my heart pounding
U   Unless you've been on the outside looking in…
S   Sisters they'll never be, friends perhaps.
I   If you were a teenager again, who would you be;
O   On the outside praying to be in.
N   Nothing else matters now.

I AM, SHE SAID

i am, she said
but what? who?
she wondered loudly
to herself.
what am I, who
am I going
to be when I
finally grow up
and not be me any
longer but that
someone else
that i don't
even recognize…

THE WAY OUT

Always looking for the way out…
    hit the light pole at 80 miles per hour – lightning!
  Fly high and away with pills and a bottle of scotch.
Jump off the roof, the bridge, back to earth.
    Head on with an 18-wheeler, dear in the headlights.
  The razor blade against the vein trick, red magic.
Walk into the ocean at night drunk – gone fishing.
    Always looking for the NEW way out…
  Send your ideas to P.O. Box 1069, Dark Night
of the Soul, Pennsylvania, 12345, with SASE
    if you want them returned.

WHATEVER!

She just doesn't get it
and probably never will
Mom's always on my case
where did my thunder
thighs come from, Anne's
aren't like that, I really
do hate her I wonder
if John will call me? I
caught him staring at
me in chemistry class
but I thought he liked
Robin I should have
polished my nails again
last night this one is
chipped and looks just
horrible maybe I should
hem my skirt a little
shorter, I hope my new
one is the right color, Oh God,
I forgot my history notes
and I really need to
study more before the
test on Friday there's
Melissa my BFF but I really
wish she wouldn't wear
that horrible pink sweater
I've tried to tell her how
bad it looks on her without
really telling her how bad
it looks on her but her
dad gave it to her and
he never gives her any
thing I bet he never
even thinks of her and

she just…I wonder about
the whole adult population
their heads are sure
screwed on backwards I
need to stop at my locker
and check my hair, make
sure nothing is caught in
my braces I hate these
things they make me uglier
then I already am and I
just know I'm gonna smile
at someone really cute one
day and there will be
something green sticking
to them or something, "Hey,
Jason!" yuck, not him, I
wonder if John will notice
the highlights, the new
lipstick, at least in this
sweater my boobs stick
out farther than my hips,
no lunch for me today
there's that snotty new
girl, Diana, she is so
gorgeous, I bet she
doesn't have one
ounce of fat anywhere
on her whole body,
I really hate her, but
she wears the dorkiest
clothes, she just
doesn't get it…
                    whatever!

FOOD FOR THOUGHT I

They devoured me in
one gulp or sometimes
many small nipping bites.
They scratched at my
very soul, piercing it
with their harsh words,
rubbing it smooth
with their lies and then
breaking off pieces of
my heart with my
own unknowing. A
feast for them, slow
starvation
for my Self and I.

FOOD FOR THOUGHT II

Ever
the
pleaser
even
with
a
broken
heart
and
a
lost
soul,
their
delicious
feast.
My
self,
crumbs.

FOOD FOR THOUGHT III

They made marks upon
my very soul, piercing
it with their harsh words,
rubbing it smooth
with their lies, and
breaking off pieces
with my unknowing.
All along it was my
self who allowed it.

*

FOOD FOR THOUGHT IV

If I allow my soul
to continue its
            spiral
of disintegration
soon there will be
nothing left but
a puff of air
where I used
            to be

FOOD FOR THOUGHT V

Finally,
  my soul rises
up,
        my body arches
in recognition,
my heart pounds
  out its story,
                finally

IN YOUR HEAD

"It's all in your head,"
            they said.
My twisted mind
replays every error
of judgment, every
nuance of shame
over and over and
over until I want to
scream in the night,
cut myself, bleed the
twisted fear right out,
tear at my eyes so I
can no longer see
into my own soul,
rip my broken and
bleeding heart from
my chest, throw it
in the dirt and watch
it pulse its life away.
Will I laugh or cry or
just walk away, one
lone tear dropping from
my left eye, splashing
like deaf thunder
on the road to glory.

You stare longingly
at the black han...
steak knife besid...
The wine in your glass w...
the candlelight as
and you forget to

The lovely, delicate,
shiny silver spoon
bowl and ornate ha...
how else would you eat so
tea, or dig a tiny h...
bury what's left of

WORDS FOR WOMEN
(AND THE MEN TOO)
EVERYWHERE...

WORDS...

you are my lover,
the interior of me.
you are me
on paper.
you are the heart
and soul of me.
you are what makes
me tick, my heart sing,
my soul expand,
my brain burst
until you come sliding,
crashing, careening,
jumping, mincing out
of me and onto
the paper
into the world
to be had by
someone else;
you are my fickle
lover, yes!

MOVING DAY

All my life I've been labeled and boxed
in by all that I presume I must be.
Little girls are seen and not heard; they
cross their ankles, are polite, genteel,
know how to succumb, how to cook and
sew and be mothers...looking back
I kept moving, labeling boxes of my own,
trying to stay one step ahead of the
insane places they wanted to stuff me
for opening my mouth one too many
times. Stay in your box, the label is
already on it, shhh child, not now.
When, I wonder, who, what, why?
The label is all scratched and no longer
legible; the box is old and falling apart.
It's been moved too many times,
closed and taped shut too often...

KITCHEN TALK

Women's voices...starved into silence.
Swallow your words and your hunger
for a life other than this.

Whispers over coffee, tea, scones.
Women, starving for connection, may
be another day.

Your tongue trips over your teeth
as you bite down harder so that the
words cannot escape.

Woman secrets, kitchen talk, so
hungry for these things – starved
into silence.

Find your voice, speak those words
before you choke on them or have
to swallow them whole again.

Your stomach expands from all the
words stuck there, turning to acid
rather than phrases.

Women's voices…starved into silence.
Swallow your words and your hunger
for a life other than this.

THE SECRET

I am a woman wrapped in a burka from early morning until late at night. I am a woman covered from head to toe in 120-degree weather. I am a woman wrapped up in a culture that despises me, spits on me, beats me, will not educate me, and refuses to allow me to even show my face outside of my own home. I know this.

I am a woman wrapped in a secret. This is the life I was born into; when I was 11 years old I decided that the revulsion, the beatings, and the being treated like chattel would not break me. But rather, it would make me stronger.

I am a woman, now 35, with a computer hidden under the living room carpet. I email. I write. I tell the world to remember me and remember all of us wrapped in our burkas; wrapped up in a society that despises our vaginas. Remember our power over the men who think they control us.

I am a woman who is making a difference for women everywhere. I am a woman who is not afraid. I know they will beat me until I no longer remember my own name and stone me until I am no more if anyone ever discovers what I am doing. I know this.

I am a woman whose mother, father, brother, aunt, sister and children would betray her to save their own family name – I know this. I am a woman who cannot stop the words from flowing. I am a woman who will never betray her sisters and who will work tirelessly to remove us all from bondage.

I am a woman wrapped in a burka who walks 20 paces behind her husband when we are out in public because that is where I belong.

I am a woman wrapped in a secret – I know where the land mines are!

A WOMAN'S PRAYER

Our sisters who are all around us
we are there for each other
in our hollowed out hallowed space
in time – we'll all see the love
that is within us,
      and without us.
This time in our lives is the
heaven that we create or
the hell that we make – our choice.
Always we will have enough,
      more than enough,
especially knowing
we have each other to give
      to and to forgive for
all the mistakes we keep making
until our hearts break with the
news that we are
      loved for ourselves,
and that is all we need to know.
So we are delivered from the evil
of thinking we are not enough
by ourselves or with each other
for the peace we make
      within our universe
multiplies the power that we are
in our own true gloriousness
if we just stay true to ourselves
and our sisters…everywhere.

amen
ah women
ah sisters
      everywhere

QUANTUM PRAYER

when I do not pray
every day I am a
      closed universe,
locked up tight upon
myself, my own
aphelion.
      And then...
when I empty my mind,
myself of all this world,
and just allow...
      I become
a supernova and the
black hole that was my
mind evolves,
      flares
and a galaxy of words
twists and turns upon
the page rather then
      turning to
            interstellar dust.

QUANTUM WOMAN I

At times I think I'm a quark,
a charmed stranger
in the star stream of life.
The black hole that is
my heart fits perfectly into
the evolved star that is myself
as I turn slowly to interstellar dust.

QUANTUM WOMAN II

The sun's brilliance is like
a supernova on the back
of my eyeballs as I slip on
dark glasses to hide from
the light that streams from
my own being…

IN THE DARK

I am a woman
     and I cry in the dark,
   where no one can see the
agony that drips like salty blood
from the corner of my eye.
It is in the dark that so many things
    happen, so much goes on in the
    absence of light, the absence of
    any sensibilities.

I am a woman
     and I cry in the dark.
   If I cried in the light, star streams
would burst out of the top of my head;
my children would run away screaming
into their own dark nights. It isn't
    the insipid, regretful, quivering
    parts of life that set me to crying
    in the dark, that make me sink
deep into the living room couch watching
the colorful bleating of the television
as it blinks and shines in rainbows,
turning my blue eyes red, green and yellow.

I am a woman
     and I cry in the dark.
   No, it is not that. It is deeper,
   uglier, a thing to be despised. It is
   the dark, shadowy part of me that I
   thought I had killed, buried long ago,
so far down it would never rise up, except
here on the other side of midnight,
     here in the dark.

I am a woman
        and I cry in the dark
      for the dead deer on the side
of the road, the leopard print clogs
outside the car in the mud puddle
left from the tsunami, the woman alone
      with nowhere to go, the scrawny cat
      crying in its own dark for a life
      undone, the three-legged dog
running on the highway and zigzagging
into the field, the Hallmark Cards commercial
that streaks across my face from the
      television that loops
           endlessly in the dark.

I am a woman
        and I cry in the dark…

I DREAM OF HORSES

Do you?
      Dream of horses I mean.
      The power of them beneath you,
      or running away from you
      into their meadow home,
      their hooves silently pounding
      the air, the ground, the air, the
      grass, the air, your heart.

It is important that you know I
      dream of horses; the silk induced
      trusting visage; their bottom-
      less pit brown eyes that guide
      me straight to their soul.

The tail that guides us into the next adventure;
      the thick tongue touching my palm
      seeking sugar cubes, apples, rainbows.
      The mane for me to hang on to when
      we race the clouds, explore the woods,
      or just canter down the dirt road to
            nowhere.

I dream of horses, do you?

LOVE IS ALL THERE IS, ISN'T IT?...

PLEASE FORGIVE ME...

The invisible bruises run deep;
the heart is broken in so many
places and mended with twine,
paper clips, tape, glue, and
embroidered with red flowers. It
will never be the same; it will
not heal true. The soul
is shriveling a little more each
year; soon it will turn to dust and
the very next sly secret may
blow it away. Then he says he's
sorry, it won't happen again, please
forgive me...as soon as that
first tear escapes and slides down
my cheek, I know what I will do,
please forgive me...

THE YEARNING HEART

What I yearn for most is to be in a loving relationship
where the inside of my soul is understood by the other;
where my heart is held in deep respect, regard and
reverence; and there is no doubt that I am "the one"
for this being.

The other in this hallowed relationship will see me for who
I really am and not run away screaming. They will see into
the deepest part of my heart, know my darkest secrets and
still look at me with unconditional love. Without flinching,
they will see into my blue eyes to the deepest caverns
below the oceans.

They will smell the wildflowers of my soul and choose to
come closer to experience all the colorful, untamed beauty.

They will touch my hand with reverence as if they have
never seen one like this; touch my cheek, chin, and eyebrow
with compassion never experienced before. They will tickle
my toes and massage my feet or lightly kiss my left
shoulder and my right earlobe.

They will taste the soft wildness of me, the sunbaked,
silvery, satin skin…what the moon might taste like on a
wintery night or the first bite of a ripe peach.

They will hear my voice and smile, inside and out. They
will hear my words and laugh, cry and know that their life
is the best it's ever been.

What I yearn for most is to be in a loving relationship where the inside of my soul is understood by the other; where my heart is held in deep respect, regard and reverence; and there is no doubt that I am "the one" for this being.

I am thinking of getting myself a dog!

WOULD THAT I COULD...

            Tell it all to you
        right from the middle
    of where I am.
            It won't work that
        way this time, however
    long I sit here.
            It's just that I
        don't even know where
    to start...too much
            has happened now,
        too many changes,
    and time,
            never a thing to
        fool with, you know.

TOGETHERNESS

Is it me you love
or the idea of me
or the idea of love;
I cannot tell
most of the time.

We kiss
without passion;
we touch barely,
never hug.

You look, but
do you see me.

I am
an image
retained on your
retina, unreal.

Last week you
looked into my
eyes, really
looked,
and as you
turned away, I
saw the fear in
yours
and felt the
tears in mine.

OUTSIDE MY WINDOW
INSIDE ME

Outside my window the sky is pale blue
overlaid by tree branches of light and shadowy greens;
the sun peeks through the leaves, winking at me.

    My soul rages; my heart gasps with forgiveness
    as I remember what I wanted to forget
    and breathe into a brand new day.

Already it is warming up; another scorcher
coming our way they say, before the storm hits
late this afternoon to turn our world upside down.

    Your image pops up in the view box in my mind,
    and instantly I smile with sweet memories forgetting
    for a moment the person you have become.

The palpable quiet of a new day is broken
by the sprinklers hissing, the birds chittering, and
cars passing on their way to the coffee shop.

    The peace within me, the self-quietude
    is disrupted as I hear you waking, and wonder
    who you are and who you will be today.

The sky is now vague lemon, anticipating, awaiting;
the clouds are gathering, talking amongst themselves,
and then conferring with the thunder and lightning.

    I watch the weather brewing, feel the storm
    mounting within me and then quickly let go
    of the emerging anger, gracefully replacing it…

MY LOVER'S HANDS...

The eyes are the windows to the soul and the hands a portrait of a personality. My lover's fingers are sinuous. His palms are like Texas, large and sprawling; his life lines a map of deep crevices and rocky roads. His nails are perfectly manicured; the little half moons lined up like good soldiers on guard.

Derek's hands know how to play my body like a priceless violin from sublime high notes to fevered crescendo. We've known each other barely a year; coming together with battle scars and hearts that have been cracked and then mended with duct tape and safety pins.

"I want to cook for you and celebrate our living together," says Derek, the wine connoisseur and suited corporate jock.

On the special night, Derek pours wine that glimmers like rubies cascading into our glasses. The ambrosia from the gourmet meal wafts around the elegant dining area.

"Delicious wine!" My tongue trips over the words as I shut the door to my doubting room and paste another smile on my gaunt face. The water glasses shimmer; the china gleams in the soft candlelit glow. The room and Derek's 6'2" frame, curly black hair and glittering gray eyes disappear as I blink, savoring the moment as if in a hallowed place.

On his way to the kitchen, his hand caresses my hair. He slides one finger slowly down my cheek and slips it under my chin to raise my lips for a brief but passionate kiss.

From the kitchen, Derek moans with ecstasy as his hands pull the roast from the oven as if it were a priceless piece of art. Before cutting into his creation, the carving artist lifts his goblet and offers a toast. "To us, to our love. May it be everlasting."

"Everlasting!"

Later, sated with food and too much drink, he declares it time for dessert. As I cut into my homemade pie, I breathe in the tangy apple mixed with the buttery crust. My mouth waters and my cheeks pucker. "For you, my love."

"Are there raisins in my apple pie? I hate raisins!" His heavy dining chair crashes to the floor as he jumps to his feet.

Stunned, a dear in the headlights of his anger, I stop breathing and watch as Derek picks up the offending piece. With his face a delicate shade of purple and his eyes thunderous, he transforms from calm to anger to rage in 10 seconds. He hurls the pie at me, like a discus thrower in the Olympics. It grazes my cheek as I bend to look for the pie knife.

His hands turn into fists and become two wrecking balls smashing into the romantic dining table. The glasses tinkle; the water wobbles in the flickering candlelight…time slows.

Derek walks towards me as if he's moving through molasses. Exhaling, I grasp the pie knife tightly and breathe deeply. I lift my head, stand my ground, and stare into Derek's stormy gray eyes as he comes closer and closer; his rage totally contained in his hands.

LONGING FOR ADVENTURE...
CHERISHING THE FAMILIAR

A piece of my heart
            is in the oven
        with the meatloaf.

It just fell off from a
            brittle edge
right into
    the meatloaf pan.

Now what do I do?
    It's the same color
as the shredded
    meat, similar texture.

My heart hurts and makes
my eyes talk
            their salty way
of things.
She is turning
away from me
            towards others.

He'll be home late
            again, another
business deal, my dear;
                he exclaims,
Sorry!

The meatloaf is burning
                    my heart.

"OH MY" MEATLOAF

2 pounds ground round
2 eggs
⅓ cup Italian bread crumbs, seasoned croutons smashed up, or one piece of whole wheat bread broken into small pieces – less dry use ¼ cup breadcrumbs.
½ small sweet onion, diced
2 cloves garlic, minced
Salt and pepper to taste
A few dashes of Worcestershire sauce
½ cup shredded cheddar cheese (could also use Asiago, Swiss, your choice)
Piece of heart optional

Combine all ingredients, except the cheese, in a medium bowl; mix well with your hands; transfer to baking pan; and form into a loaf. Make an indentation/channel down the center of the loaf; pour in the cheese; and close up the meat around the cheese. Bake with love at 350 degrees until your desired doneness – about 45 min. for medium. Serves 4-5.

THE DINNER PARTY

Your hand shakes slightly
　　　　as you lift the fork to your mouth
　　　　carefully balancing a row of peas.
As you part your lips, he says, too loudly
　　　　for your mind to bend into, "I
　　　　don't love you anymore."

You stare longingly
　　　　at the black handled, keen edged
　　　　steak knife beside your dirty dinner plate.
The wine in your glass wobbles in
　　　　the candlelight as a tear threatens,
　　　　and you forget to breathe.

The lovely, delicate,
　　　　shiny silver spoon with smooth shallow
　　　　bowl and ornate handle, so useful, so
　　　　wanted, necessary;
how else would you eat soup, sugar your
　　　　tea, or dig a tiny hole in the dirt to
　　　　bury what's left of your heart?

THE LOVE LETTER

Faded ink,
        a miasmic stream of
                forgotten words,
scratched and scrawled on a
        now wrinkled, hopeless, worn
                out sheet of paper.

I remember
        when it was crisp, new, whiter
                than the first snow,
brighter than a July day,
        ready for anything.
                Where are the others?

Bundled, tied tightly
        with a yellow ribbon, carefully
                saved like the love we
grasped and squeezed the life
        from without knowing what
                we were doing.

A solitary, salty drop
        turns sentences into smeary
                lines which rush madly
for the sides of the paper.
        My heart is a passion fruit
                split in two.

CHARLIE – THE LOVE OF MY LIFE

I've been in love before, but not like this.

Charlie is different from all the others, and I know he unconditionally loves me. I can see it in his golden brown, sunshiny eyes. We're totally tuned into each other, and we've only been together for 18 months. Sometimes he seems to know what I am thinking. I love his long red hair, his lithe muscular body, and his quick intelligence. Charlie is unique.

We spend a lot of time together and never tire of each other. As a semi-retired marketing entrepreneur working from an extra room in my house, my time is flexible, so on some days we could be together all day.

Charlie seems to have an intuitive sense about my emotional states…how many other males can you say that about? Let me give you an example. One day last week I was having computer challenges, had project deadlines, and nothing was going right. I was literally pounding the computer keys and muttering to myself when Charlie peeked into my office; then he quickly retreated to another room when I shook my head and struck my fist on the desk in frustration. He wisely, quietly went back downstairs.

Later while readying for my appointment, I turned everything off, grabbed the documents I needed and ran downstairs. I gathered my car keys, water and sunglasses then leaned over to place things in my briefcase. Immediately, I burst into tears and gales of laughter at the same time.

Right inside at the top of my briefcase was a silk flower. The only place I have silk flowers is in the guest bedroom upstairs arranged in a bowl on the dresser. I had been alone in the house all day with Charlie. The flower had *not* been in my briefcase earlier when I went upstairs to do battle with my computer.

His instinctive thoughtfulness changed my day in an instant. I hugged Charlie and thanked him profusely.

He stared at me with golden-eyed independence then flounced away; his long, bushy cat tail high in the air. He was off to plan his next bit of fun; solve a difficult calculus problem; plot to overthrow the government; or take another nap.

I ran out the door wiping the tears from my eyes and giving the world my 1000-watt smile. I now know why people leave their whole inheritance to their cat.

QUANTUM LOVE I

Before this, I was
just zodiacal light;
I stare at you with
star stream eyes,
wondering if you see
me or are just caught
up in the black hole
that is my heart. Our
love feels like a
starburst galaxy, or
are we in a flare star
state soon to turn
to interstellar dust?
Or worse, back to
                normal…

QUANTUM LOVE II

You are my sun, moon, stars,
and I am your aphelion. You
are my rad, and I am your
flare star as I watch and
hope that our love evolves
rather than turn to interstellar
dust!

LIFE ON THE
OTHER SIDE
OF MIDNIGHT...

LEARNING TO RIDE A BIKE

climb on,
        fall off
get on
  fall off
climb back on
        thinking…
this time I won't
  fall off
of course,
you
        fall off
and of course,
you
        get back on…
just like life…it
  doesn't matter
        how many times you
fall off, what counts
        is the times you
        get back on…

BACKSTAGE EARLY MORNING

this morning, the angels
haven't turned the lights on yet.
quietly, the gunmetal sky
slips into a clean white shirt,
buttoning it up tight...then
from stage left the horizon
jumps into her hot pink ballerina
skirt, whirling, pirouetting, teetering
on Mother Earth's shoulder, to
throw purple ribbons into the
silver sky, laughing gaily as she
crosses; then fades into the
orchestra pit of another day.
the still weary sky knots his blue
striped tie and pulls up charcoal
gray pants
          morning begins...

MORNING GLORY MUFFINS

(Makes 12 – from my dear friend Ms. Gus)

In a large bowl, combine dry ingredients:
1	cup flour
1	cup your choice – whole wheat flour, cornmeal, wheat germ, oatmeal
½	cup brown sugar
1	Tbsp baking powder
1	tsp cinnamon
½	tsp salt

Make a well in the center and add:
⅓	cup oil
1	egg – beat with a fork within the well
1	cup liquid of your choice – milk, soy milk, yogurt, applesauce

Add 3-4 handfuls of etceteras – your choice – shredded carrots, apples, raisins, craisins, coconut, seeds, apricots; can use frozen fruit, walnuts, pecans or your nut choice. If your etceteras are sweet, cut back on the sugar; if wet, cut back on the liquid. If using canned pumpkin, add pumpkin spice; if ginger-bready, add molasses, cocoa and chocolate chips, etcetera. Bake at 400 degrees for 30 minutes.

IT'S YOUR JOURNEY, YOU KNOW

Focused on work, family, big trucks,
fast motorcycles, making more money,
and the current deal, he never stopped
to smell the roses along the way. The
malignancy buried deep in his gray
matter is small but growing aggressively.
He has 12-18 months give or take a
minute or two. We'll try surgery
tomorrow but probably won't get it
all. Then radiation. We'll let you know.

Focused on the delicacies across
the road, he never saw the SUV that
suddenly flattened him from mid-
back to the tip of his bushy squirrel
tail. He completes his journey slowly,
tortuously, pulling himself across the
roadway by his front paws. His little
mouth is open in a silent scream. I know.

Focused on living life, having fun,
doing things her way she never heard
how loud her biological clock was
ticking. He was kind, handsome and
lived every day with a life threatening
illness. They met, fell in love, married
and desperately wanted children. Don't
worry; you have three more tries. The
doctors feel confident. The next time
everything will be right. They just know.

Focused on his corporate career, golf,
drinking beer with the guys, he almost
never touched her, kissed her, hugged
her anymore. Starved, unhappy, wanting
more from the person who said he
loved her, she disappeared into her own
future to love and live to the fullest. He still
wonders why she left. "I gave her gifts,
took her out to eat. Women! I don't know!"

Focused on all the to-dos that never really
matter anyway she ate alone, quickly at
the kitchen counter. Another bowl of cold
cereal is just fine. Why cook a whole meal
just for myself? What's the point? I want to
taste more of life instead of the spices I
put in my chili. I miss her away at college,
and him just married and happily on his own.
Now what?! Mom always said, "you'll know."

TWO WEEKS OF TORTURE IN A TENT
SUBTITLE: SUMMER CAMP

Shoot me right now and put me
immediately out of my misery.
If one more spider hides in my
shoe, if one more mosquito bites
my body, if one more rain drop
leaks through the tent, I may not
make it out of here alive. I
didn't know my parents hated
me this much.

Shoot me now so that I don't
have to listen to the other girls
whispering, laughing at me
since I'm the new kid at camp,
and so I don't have to jump into
the lake of ice water and swim to
the raft that is at least 20 miles away.
I won't make it; my arms are too
scrawny. I'll be a red cap forever,
stuck with the kids half my age.

Shoot me now so I can get out
of today's adventure in the woods,
so I can go back home to the
familiar concrete neighborhood
where I'm outgoing and fun. Here
my feet get tangled up, my
tongue gets tied in knots, my
stomach is constantly lurching.
I would hide under my cot
and never come out, but it's
too scary under there.

Shoot me now so that I can go
up to heaven with my Nana since
being here has given me a taste
of hell. I promise to be a very
good girl for the rest of my life,
if I live through the next 9 days.
I've only been here 4 days, 6 hours
and 29 minutes!?…Shoot me now!

FRUITS OF TECHNOLOGY

blackberry in hand,
the manager emails his office
from his seat on the toilet,
early morning business.

apple on my table,
fingers flashing over keyboard
peering at the laptop screen,
seeds of thought from the core.

blackberry pressed to your ear
as you hurry along busy city streets
talking to your college daughter,
patched together across the miles.

apples in the classroom
gifts for the children, learning early
how to be technologically savvy,
byte by delicious byte.

LOVE AND GRACE

Love is a sunset
>Grace is the sunrise

Love is the feel of a single rose petal
>Grace is the thorn

Love is looking at myself in the mirror
>Grace is not getting startled

Love is the vice grip of a newborn's fist on your finger
>Grace is that the newborn is your grandchild

Love is becoming the "I am" of who I imagined
>Grace is realizing it

Love is having a happy, healthy, 30-something son
>Grace is him saying, "I love you, mom" from his corporate cubicle

Love is still gasping at the NYC skyline after 50 years
>Grace is never forgetting

Love is early morning as the earth holds its breath…
>Grace is the sun bursting on the horizon!

THE YELLOW QUILT
It's All In The Family – Until…

MARY – the beginning…the grandmother

How could she…?

She watched her four children with a smile that never made it to her vacant, stormy sea-gray eyes. As if an elephant sat on her thick shoulders, she gently shepherded her three young girls and the baby boy into the large, bright kitchen. The sweet goodness of the freshly baked oatmeal raisin cookies filled the air, which made her pale cheeks puff and her lips pout with anticipation. *That no good husband of mine only likes chocolate chip cookies, she ruminated to herself.*

How could she…?

On the floor she carefully spread the yellow quilt, the one with the star pattern that her grandmother had made for her. It was a wedding gift – that long ago and faraway ceremony. *I know he's going to leave me soon. That no account fool. Good riddance, she thought.*

How could she…?

"Hold tight to your favorite dollies," she advised as the girls chattered, chatted and giggled together on the quilt. "Here is your favorite toy truck," she said to her baby son as she checked his diaper. The salty sadness trickled then cascaded silently from those stormy eyes as she patted the soft wisps of hair on his sweet-baby-smelling head.

"We're going to have a kitchen picnic today before Daddy gets home!" *He'll be sorry!*

82

She smoothed out the dress of her oldest daughter, who is almost ten years old now. She gently positioned the collar on the middle sister's carefully ironed blouse and pulled up the left sock one more time on the six-year-old.

How could she...?

She handed each of her children a warm, fresh baked cookie; each a nugget of sweetness gripped to crumbling in their tiny hands. *I'll show him, she declared to no one but the anxious voices in her head.*

As the girls pulled their brother close and played happily together, she placed a thick layer of her best blue towels at the bottom of the kitchen door. She double and triple checked the windows. Slowly moving as if through a river of molasses, she went to the stove, blew out the pilot light, and turned on all four burners and the oven. *That fool, she muttered.*

How could she...?

"How long will it take?" she wondered as she sat down next to her children on the pretty yellow quilt. A raisin dropped unnoticed on her red gingham apron that covered her pendulous breasts when she brought the sugary warm cookie, as if in slow motion, to her full lips and took a large bite.

How could she...?

MARGARET – next in line...the mother

Could she...?

Alone, pacing the desolate New York winter beach, the wind whips through her straight black hair and plasters it to her red, raw face. She tries to turn away from the icy, needle poking winds spritzing salty spray into her already saltier eyes that are the same color as the green-gray ocean that mists and swirls around her.

Could she…?

She wraps the pale yellow quilt tighter around her broad shoulders and burrows deeper into the one bright spot in the colorless seascape. Icy tendrils from the sea slide down the neck of her coat, dripping, slipping down her spine. She shivers; she is chilled to the frozen marrow of her bones. The sun has been a stranger for many days now. *I wish that handsome husband of mine was here with me at such a delicate time instead of off fighting a faraway war. Maybe he'll disappear like my father, she ponders.*

Could she…?

Alone and lonely she trudges as if through quicksand; she is battling her own internal wars. She is slowly veering towards the explosion of the wintery sea's angry surf as it bombards the shore. She veers closer. *Maybe it's time to lean into the water and get lost* in those wandering waves beckoning to her, beckoning, calling to her…the cold breaking, beating, tom-tom of never-ending waves. The yellow quilt trails behind her; it drags wet sand in its wake as it makes unearthly patterned whorls.

Could she…?

Looking up at the seagulls screeching above, she is jealous. She wants to screech and holler and let the world know how terrified she is. She wants to join the seagulls and fly away to some far-off sunny place; she aches to fly away to another space in time where she would not be carrying this extra burden. *He'll never know.* Now, looking down at the swell of her body with much more than shells and sand growing inside her, feeling pinned to this earth, she veers closer and closer to the breaking waters. *I feel so old and so very tired...*

Could she...?

She feels the icy water slosh over the tops of her sensible shoes; it squishes between her toes as she wriggles them inside the brown leather. The yellow quilt floats and undulates regally on the waves around her as she takes her next step.

Could she...?

FRANCES – the current one...the daughter

She...?

...lost herself in the urgent need to be thinner than a piece of paper or a blade of grass. A ghostly, wispy sliver shivering in the night, she wraps the now not-so-bright yellow quilt around her disappearing bony frame as she paces back and forth across the lightless room. *What more must I do?* she wonders.

She...?

...is pregnant. She has to have him (she knows it's a him...a woman's intuition has always been better than a machine) very soon. Her beloved mother-in-law is slowly wasting away too but from the cancer cells that consistently rampage her already ravaged body. The acid flowing in her veins is not stopping that army of invaders; the cells march on destroying everything in their path. She wants to see this first grandchild before she breathes her last breath.

She…?

I did my best. (This wasn't the era of Skype, cell phone photos, or instant anything.) My sweet mother-in-law never got to see the indigo blue eyes just like hers; the cap of bright carrot hair just like hers; or the brown blotches of freckles that would one day cover his body just like hers. *I did my best, but it wasn't good enough,* she thought as a lone tear escapes from her right eye and runs silently, quickly down her cheek; the droplet disappears into her neck.

She…?

…stops her endless pacing around the well-appointed living room and gazes at her sweet, sleeping, perfect baby boy. With his right hand curled into a miniature fist, his rosebud lips move as if he's giving a speech in his dreams. He smells like soap, powder and all that is good about a healthy baby. He just fell asleep on this lazy, hazy fall afternoon. *This time, I hope it works,* she says to the empty house.

She…?

…looks one more time at her baby boy, where she has placed him on the faded yellow quilt on the floor of the living room. *He'll be safe right here*, she thinks, *and his dad will be home in an hour so the timing should be perfect.* She empties the bottle of pills (the yellow ones that the doctor gave her since she can't be happy anymore) into her shaking, skeletal hand and pops them all at once into her mouth.

She…?

…swallows them down with a glass of whiskey. Choking, coughing, and swallowing hard to make sure they stay down; she gulps another glass full of the burning amber liquid. Like a hot poker, it courses its way down her throat. "I love you my sweet, sweet, darling boy. I love you more than you can ever imagine…" she says as she lies down next to her baby and pushes her emaciated finger inside his tiny fist. *"I love you so much…! More than life itself!" She…?*

RYAN – her son, another beginning…

He…

That red-haired baby is all grown up now, married, living and working in New York City; he is dreaming of a son of his own one day. He and his wife just bought a tan buttery leather sofa and are proudly sending instant photos to everyone, posting it on their Facebook page, and everything else young people are wont to do.

He…

A package arrives in the mail a few weeks later containing three obviously handmade pillows. The antique background fabric is a faded pale yellow; it has been embellished with beads, embroidered trees, and flowers in tans, greens, golds, and bright yellows to symbolize growth and all that is beautiful. They perfectly match the sofa.

He…

"These are beautiful!" he exclaims to his wife who agrees with an ear-to-ear grin as she carefully, almost reverentially places them on the sofa. *My mom is so amazing and I'm glad she's happy these days. Maybe doing her art like these pillows helps…* he thinks to himself.

"Your mom is so thoughtful. These pillows with the embroidered flowers and trees make everything look alive and so pretty," she says. "But, that pale yellow background fabric looks so familiar…" she adds. "Didn't she have a quilt like this at one time?"

"Could be…"

He…

WALK A MILE
IN THESE SHOES

THE BROWN OXFORD

The flashing lights screamed silently on the red-and-white ambulance that came for him on the other side of midnight last week. His 96-year-old heart had given out. No amount of pounding on his hairless white chest, polka-dotted with brown age spots shaped like Massachusetts, was going to bring a smile to his round, florid face.

Never again will I be able to see the twinkle in his startlingly sea-blue eyes as we share stories from long ago. Why didn't I bring over some homemade soup, a piece of my birthday cake last month, or the new book by that author he loved? I had it right here by the front door, ready. I thought we had all the time in the world. What was the hurry?

Safe in my living room vantage point from across the street, I watch his runway-thin granddaughter with his same shocking eyes saunter up the walk to his front door as if someone is watching her every move. She hesitates and then falls to her knees on the top step of his porch; her head bows as if in prayer. Her waist-length hair slips around her like a curtain made from a family of ravens with blue-black translucent wings blowing in the light, spring breeze.

Her whole body shakes, as if a hand has ascended from Middle-earth to twist and contort her slight frame. *What happened?* Mesmerized, I stare at her; then my glance slides over her shoulder and follows her hand as it touches his single well-made, but weary and worn, scuffed brown Oxford lying on its side, forlorn, forgotten, in front of the wooden porch rocker.

THE SNEAKER

As if stroking the wing of a butterfly, I gently touch the frayed, broken lace and the bumpy place where a tiny knot kept it together. The rubber on the right side has a black scuff mark darker than the other side of midnight. On the canvas top, I stick my finger in a hole the size of a gnats wing. I swallow, almost choking, on the sob that threatens.

I withdraw my hand, quickly, as memories burn like a candle flame. Held together with superglue, sealing wax and a few knots of its own, another piece of my heart breaks off and disappears.

This tiny piece of a long-ago life fits in the palm of my hand with room to spare. Where is the mate to this remnant from yesterday, the partner in all those childhood games? What happened to that little boy who long ago disappeared into the man who now dreams of a son of his own?

THE PENNY LOAFER

Next to the reddish-brown loafer, with the penny still peeking from its secret spot up front, is a lone, forlorn letter. A miasmic stream of faded, forgotten words is scratched and scrawled on a now wrinkled, hopelessly worn-out sheet of paper.

I remember when it was crisp, new, whiter than the first snowstorm, brighter than a July day, and ready for anything. Where are the others? Are they bundled, choked with a yellow ribbon, and carefully saved like the love we grasped and squeezed the life from without knowing what we were doing?

I wonder where the other penny loafer has gone as I touch the once shiny piece of copper and jerk my hand away as memories burn to ignite the shame in my heart. My mind bends as I rub the coin with my shirt hoping to restore its former shine and luster. My heart knows that this cannot happen.

THE HIGH TOP

Being fourteen is the worst. I'll never have a boyfriend. My nose it too big. I'll be flat-chested my whole life and totally unlovable. I may never get my period; Anne, Karen and Linda got theirs when they were eleven. My best friend Melissa hasn't called all week. I wonder if she's mad at me.

I'm already fourteen and nothing good ever happens to me. How could God make earth such a miserable place to live? I know I did horrible on that algebra test. I just don't get it. I am such a failure; what's the point of going on? I just don't get it! It's so nasty outside, gray and sleety. I don't think the sun will ever shine again…the world will just stay colorless like being in the middle of a perpetual thunderstorm. Just like me.

Now I can't find my other high-top running shoe. WTF! Being fourteen is *the* very worst. Where is my other shoe? Why can't I find my other shoe? I wonder if someone took it.

Now I've done it! Losing my temper and throwing things seems to be what I do best. And, of course, it just had to hit my favorite and only framed vintage Smashing Pumpkins poster and shatter the glass. Just like my life…Where the hell is my other shoe?

FAITH AND THE NEW RUNNING SHOES

Hebrews 11:1 "Now faith is the assurance of things hoped for, the conviction of things not seen."

The pea-soupy misty morning moves on cat feet as I pick up my pace and try to out run Mother Nature and the truckload of cotton balls she has dumped around me. As I run along the Jersey side of the haughty Hudson River, the flimsy, fine particles of condensed water vapor are like soupy sleet stuck in midair, yet lighter than the flap of a butterfly wing on my cheek, obscuring the railing that shields the concrete byway above the river.

The world is still and strange wrapped in a sleepy but startling silence. The slap-shush, slap-shush, slap-shush of my running shoes on the concrete path are the only un-sounds this morning.

What is behind this foggy curtain? I shove my fist into the everlasting, enveloping dew expecting to bruise my knuckles on something tangible. Will I touch an alien presence, the monster that used to hide under my bed, or something slippery and slimy? My hand disappears into the thick air meeting no resistance. Trying another tactic, I stick out my tongue as if this mountain of cotton candy beside me might be sweet.

Is it the bustling New York metropolis that was there last night or just the river stretching to the Atlantic and silently slipping out to sea…or nothing? Is the world wrapped in this gauzy nothing everything-ness, or am I?

As I round the bend and begin the slight hill climb, an acrid burning scent hangs in the air like a child on a swing; it is assaulting me, tickling the inside of my nose, and making my throat close up. It's almost like the incense from childhood, but not. The residue of burned leaves is a reminder that autumn is almost used up as winter winds wobble in from the north. The thin dew laden autumn air will soon turn to icy cubed crystallized air. Then I can wear my new high-topped, thick-soled winterized running shoes.

All these thoughts fade into the background of my mind as I turn my head to the right and wonder...

THE PROPERTIES OF WATER AND
THE LEOPARD PRINT CLOG

A drop of water between life and death is sustenance for our bodies which are fifty-seven percent water. Frozen, water keeps your cocktail cold; heated up, it makes your coffee and tea or boils your eggs, pasta, and soup. Luxuriate in its scented warmth, turn on the kitchen tap or walk ten miles to find fresh water. Swim in it; drown in it. Get trampled by the beautiful, heavenly turquoise-blue ocean that has turned into a watery wall bearing down relentlessly.

News item one week after the tsunami in Japan:

Mrs. Sang and her husband of 25 years are currently living in their late model sedan parked in a few inches of muddy, filthy water on a suburban street. Their house disappeared last week in the wall of water that roared, galloped and turned so suddenly into a steam locomotive that many had no time to breathe, much less get out of the way.

Following the spiritual tradition of no shoes in the "house," a pair of leopard print clogs floats atop the putrid water outside the passenger door of the car.

What's that floating by the driver's door?

IF THAT BLACK LEATHER HIGH-HEELED BOOT COULD TALK!

"Hurry up! It's getting late and your *darling* fiancé will be home any minute. We have got to hurry, please!"

"Don't you think *I* know that? Sorry, sorry, I didn't mean to snap at you. I have never been more frightened in my life."

"Well, that makes two of us. How much more do you have?"

"This is the last bag of my clothes. We already have my favorite chair, books, dishes and sewing machine. You take this, and I'll walk through the rest of the apartment to make sure I didn't forget anything."

"We can buy whatever you might have missed…There are about a million butterflies whirling around inside my stomach. They must be having a party or something. Let's go!" Barb says, staring down at her watch.

"I'll catch up with you. Give me one more minute…I need to straighten up things so it doesn't look so obvious that I'm gone. Maybe at first he won't even notice…" Marla says.

"You're lying to yourself again…but you're good at that, Marla. And so is you-know-who."

"I know, I know, I kn…" Marla sobs. "Barb, what am I going to do?"

"You are going to follow me out this door. We are getting into our cars. You are following me down the street and across town to your new apartment, your new life, your new you. That is what you are going to do. If you want to make a statement, dump those damned apology roses in the garbage where he can see them. The thing you are *not* going to do is look back with doubt or anything else in your eyes. You cannot. You do not have that luxury right now. Please, Marla, hurry up!"

She's right; I know she's right but...I thought he was "the one." He was so sweet, so loving, and so romantic before I moved in with him. I thought we would be married, have children, grow old together and live happily ever after...ha! I remember the night he proposed...get going, Marla!

I take the ring from my finger and gently place it on his dresser. *"Barb is right. I cannot look back. It might be the last time,"* I think as I wince when I blink my swollen, bruised eye.

With a soul-wrenching sob and a shake of her head, Marla limps out the door.

Lying in the hallway near their bedroom door, a black leather, lace-up high-heeled boot is all that remains.

IT IS WHAT IT IS...

discover

101

TIME CHANGE

Some are taken
        aback
never quite ad-
justed to the
clock, a fore-
shadow of their
        life.
Others keep
moving ahead
marching to
their own
        beat.
Time is in their
Favor; change is.

CHARLIE THE ALARMING CAT

Charlie, my beloved Maine Coon wonder, seems to be Einstein-smart. I feel like the class dunce sometimes when Charlie cocks his tabby-colored, bushy head, looks at me with his flecked, golden eyes, and meows long and low. He knows exactly what he wants – it is I, the human, who has no clue.

"What is it, Charlie?" I innocently ask.

"Meeoowww, meow, meow," he replies as he meanders into the kitchen and stands in front of the refrigerator. He looks at me as if to say, *"what I love is in that big box and if I had opposable thumbs I would get it myself, but unfortunately, I must rely on humans. You specifically in the morning since you are the early riser. Thank you very much!"*

"When I want my head scratched, I sit quietly peering at you over my shoulder, and if I want a full-out belly rub, I lie on my back with my paws in the air. When I am hungry, I sit nonchalantly in front of the big box until you get the message. You humans…I swear!"

"Oh, and you coo at me and talk baby talk, which by the way sounds ridiculous. I'm almost four, which in your world would be possibly 24; this means if I was human I would have graduated from college and be working full time – just sayin'. So you really could talk to me the way you talk to your human friends. It would be less demeaning also, you know. As long as you rub my belly, I guess I can put up with the cooing though."

"Getting back to mornings…I am HUNGRY. If I was allowed to go out those big glass doors in that room

with the big table with the chairs all around it, I know I could find my own food, but I'm an 'inside cat'. Whoopee!"

Charlie certainly is hungry in the mornings, to that I can attest. He starts his meowing at 5:30, like an alarm clock right on schedule.

"Well, of course it's the same time every day. Do the birds, squirrels and rabbits sleep in? What, are you kidding me? Mother Nature starts waking all those creatures up at about 5:00 and that's when I start prowling around the house. I just don't make a lot of noise. I eat some dry food, but I really, really want what's in that big metal box. So when my stomach is rumbling and my mouth is itchy, I just have to wake you up. It's the law – Charlie's and Mother Nature's law."

When his internal clock rings, Charlie comes to the side of my bed and begins his plaintive cries. When I just turn over and ignore him, he walks silently on those big cushioned cat feet and jumps on my dresser. Once there, he starts pushing things off onto the floor. If the banging and crashing doesn't make me move, he starts chewing on my earrings hanging on the jewelry tree. That gets…

"That gets her up! It's not the noise, you know. She just thinks I'm going to hurt those colorful, silly looking baubles…I can tell when I bite into them that they're not real gold, so what's she worried about anyway? I'll bet she can't even see those teeth marks."

One morning I was really tired. It was Monday and I just didn't want to get up when Charlie meowed at the side of my bed. When I looked at the clock and the green luminescent numbers screamed 5:32, I said to Charlie, "please sweet cat, come back in 30 minutes and then I'll get up and fix your breakfast, I promise."

At 6:02, there was Charlie at the side of my bed.

"Meow, meeeooooowww meow!"

When I saw those shiny numbers saying 6:02, my eyes popped open and I looked at Charlie as I jumped out of bed...exactly 30 minutes, how did he do that?

"What, are you kidding me? I am Charlie, the alarming cat."

LUNCH FOR AN ANOREXIC

Appetizer: 1 teaspoon low-fat cottage cheese with walnut
　　　　on top
　　　　Calories:　　　24

Coffee: one cup, black
　　　　Calories:　　　0

Salad Course: 3 lettuce leaves, 1 cherry tomato, 1 very
　　　　thin slice of cucumber, 1 baby carrot, hold the
　　　　croutons, oil and vinegar dressing
　　　　Calories:　　　13

Coffee: one cup, black
　　　　Calories:　　　0

Main Course: tuna salad sandwich – 1 teaspoon tuna,
　　　　a pinch of salt and pepper to taste, hold the mayo –
　　　　served between 2 water table crackers
　　　　Calories:　　　32

Dessert: as many cups of coffee as desired – black
　　　　Calories:　　　0

　　　　Total Calories: 69

And, what will you have?

I think I'll just have a cup of coffee. I'm not very hungry.

A good time was had by all!

EVERYTHING I KNOW I LEARNED FROM MY CAT...

(Written by a human – or so she thinks – come on, folks. Do you really think humans have this kind of knowledge? I don't need opposable thumbs to type on a keyboard. It takes me a little longer but...)

My cat Charlie knows:

Feigned indifference – how to get the person in your life to pay attention to you and do what you want – simple and this goes for anyone, so listen up. Walk away. Do not run. Turn slowly with a sly smile just beginning to break on to your lips, toss your head but ever so slightly and slowly, v-e-r-y s-l-o-w-l-y, walk away as if this is *the* most natural thing you do and that you do it all the time – walk away.

Do not, under any circumstances, look back – *EVER.* Keep walking. If they catch up to you, call out to you or come close to you, turn slowly and look at them with a tilt of your head...as if to say – "Are you talking/touching/calling out to me!?" Wait, head still slightly cocked; do not allow your heart to leap up into your eyes or your throat at all...keep your cool, even if the fire in your belly (or lower) is blazing, and say *nothing*.

Stay cool – you are a cool cat. That is all your brain should be saying right now...("I am a cool cat"- repeat after me, "I am a cool cat" and keep repeating, "I am a cool cat," until you believe it.) Then, look away as if you have no interest. Feigned indifference. Felines are masters at this. It works every time – not just once in a while but *EVERY* time!!! You will get anything your little heart desires. Any object of your affection will be yours. I guarantee it.

Get exactly what you want now – the operative word is *now* – immediately – like right away. You just keep asking (in my case meowing plaintively) until one of them wakes up and gets it for you. If I had opposable thumbs, I'd do it myself. I would not have to rely on anyone or anything, especially those humans. Didn't I make myself abundantly clear? – then why can't she just get me what I'm asking for?

If I want you to scratch my belly, I will lie on the floor (or the rug) with my belly exposed; I don't do this lightly – exposed is the operative word here. I am totally vulnerable and we do not like to be vulnerable in any way. That is how I am more like the humans, but I don't let it bother me, change my personality or get to me – I just get the belly rub and move on – it's back to basics and being very simple – one more time.

You must be clear – abundantly, morbidly, totally clear and you will get it every time. I know what I want – water from the faucet, food from the big black box, or more food and TREATS from that little room that has shelves and shelves of all good things to eat.

Everything in life is quite simple. It's the humans that complicate everything. There is no need for that.

NEW SKY 13,500

Endless cerulean blue,
no clouds
to lose myself in
on this fall day,
the intense cold,
icy, nipping at my ears,
biting through
the layers I wear,
no protection from this
vast intense sky of life
that flash freezes
my very heart.
Suddenly, a bird chirps
appearing as if from nowhere
and then gone in a
quick blink of one sky-blue eye.
The earth is rising
in its brown, green, redness
with black snake roads
winding endlessly, slithering everywhere.

With a quick tug
the world and I stand still
for one instant in time,
one never ending frozen moment.
I float in the vast blueness,
a microcosmic spec of life;
nothing and everything
all at the same time.
The quiet is what I hear the most;
my soul implodes
as my mind wraps around
the beauty that is our Mother.

As my feet touch the Technicolor grass,
I sidestep a fading fall flower,
realizing each is perfect
in its own way.
As are we all.

I AM A WEAVER

I AM A WEAVER
With a ball of sunny yellow yarn,
   a variegated skein of soft
      moss green and pastel pink,
        and one of bright royal blue;
      two more of orange and crimson;
one with a touch of violet.
   I weave something magical
      infused with happiness and love
   that might make you smile when you see it,
as you reach out a wondering hand
     to touch so tenderly.

I AM A WEAVER
Unraveling my life, thread, by thin, barely
   recognizable thread; severing the fearful,
     sad, depressed and suicidal ones.
    I am discarding the angry,
  blaming, shaming, judging,
guilt-ridden strands; forever letting go of the
   loveless, joyless threads that have been
     part of me for too long now.

I AM A WEAVER
I have knubbly, electric blue threads
   of being true to myself,
     knowing I am enough. Woven in tabby,
     plain, simple yet strongly reliable,
      like the voice I am trying on…
true, strong and filled with integrity.
    Sunflower-yellow strands of self forgiveness
      mixed with a bumpy deep ochre yarn

for forgiveness of others are
 woven in a daisy chain with endless loops
 doubling back on themselves.

I AM A WEAVER
Layers of orange are next in a very
 intricate pattern of over-and-under,
 reworked delicately back in rows
 that are purposely uneven;
not perfect but so intriguing to the eye.
 This is the creative part of me –
 the writer, the artist, the fiercely,
 fearless creative one;
whole and showing up at long last.

I AM A WEAVER
Smooth silky, fine, thin green and pink
 variegated yarn that represents love.
 Love of and for self, for two and
 four-legged others, the trees, flowers,
and all of Mother Nature. Love for the planet.
 Although plain, smooth, serene,
 its very loveliness makes your fingers twitch,
 yearning to reach out and rub the
silky, smooth, endless loops of love and kindness,
 knowing you will find comfort there.

I AM A WEAVER
Shades of lavender, violet and purple
 grace the top of this fine tapestry;
 strands woven in a pattern more intricate
 than the inner landscape of a single rose;
unspun wool gathered together in soft, cloudlike,
 formless shapes that have
 a definite place in this scheme.

Smooth, bumpy, formless, then
smooth again in a pattern all its own.
This is part inner peace, part outer peace,
with a small amount of world peace mixed in.

I AM A WEAVER
I am a work of art in progress. I may always be so.
I feel my life right now to be a magical adventure,
filled with non-judgmental, forgiving, joyful,
outrageous, audacious, loving energy;
you might smile when you happen upon my rewoven self;
although you may not know why.
I am weaving something wonderful,
beautiful, awesome and true.

I AM A WEAVER
Re-weaving me.

A BRAND NEW WORLD

when I awakened this morning
the dreams had escaped,
but I had not.
everything was the same, yet,
totally different;
something happened in the night.
I am not the same person
who lay her head on the
feather pillow the night before.
it is elusive, curious and amazing;
fruitful in its splendor,
tender in its simplicity.
to put a finger on it
is not possible since
fingers do not go that deep
inside one's psyche,
into the center
of the heart storm;
the soul search to the
broken parts that might never
be whole.   until now…
                    THE BEGINNING…

ACKNOWLEDGMENTS

This book would not be if not for all my women friends who have stood by me in life as well as all my iterations as a writer. Thank you to the three dear friends (Linda B., Linda P. and Niki) who read this book and inspired me to keep going. Special thanks to Maggie Pund, the remarkable genius who edited the essays, formatted the pages and boosted this book into being. Thank you one and all.

Made in the USA
Columbia, SC
28 November 2018